Sam Sits

Written by Alex Marson

Illustrated by Andrew Painter

Collins

Sit Sam!

sit sit sit

Dad pats Sam.

pat pat pat

Sit in it Sam!

6

Sam sits in it.

Sit Sam! Sam sits.

Nan pats Sam.

Sam pats it.

Sam sits in it!

Sam sits in it.

Sam naps in it.

14

After reading

Letters and Sounds: Phase 2

Word count: 44

Focus phonemes: /s/ /a/ /t/ /p/ /i/ /n/ /m/ /d/

Curriculum links: Understanding the world; PSED

Early learning goals: Reading: read and understand simple sentences; use phonic knowledge to decode regular words and read them aloud accurately

Developing fluency

- Your child may enjoy hearing you read the book.
- Take turns to read a page with your child beginning on page 2 so that they can read the speech bubble too. Check your child pauses between sentences.

Phonic practice

- Turn to page 4 and sound out each word together. (D/a/d   p/a/t/s   S/a/m) Ask: Which word has the /d/ sound? (*Dad*)
- On page 9, focus on the /n/ and /m/ sounds. Read the sentence together. Ask your child: Which word has the /n/ sound? (*Nan*) Which word has the /m/ sound? (*Sam*)
- Look at the "I spy sounds" pages (14 and 15). Point to and sound out the /d/ at the top of page 14, then point to the duck picture and say "ducks", emphasising the /d/ sound. Take turns to find an item in the picture that starts with the /d/ sound. (*Dad, doughnuts, dog, drums, dates, drink*) Can your child find words with the /d/ sound in the word, and not at the beginning? (*window, clouds*)

Extending vocabulary

- Turn to pages 6 and 7 and discuss words you could use to describe the aliens. Focus on the picture on page 6. What words could describe Dad? (e.g. *two horns, one eye, stripy tie*) What words describe Mum? (*one horn, spots and stripes, necklace, smaller teeth*). Repeat for Nan on page 9.